Friday 28ᵗʰ April 4·10

THE FABER EASY-PLAY KEYBOARD SERI

PLAY ROMANTIC
RUSSIA

arranged for easy keyboard
by David Mather and Daniel Scott

FABER MUSIC

Contents

© 1989 by Faber Music Ltd
First published in 1989 by Faber Music Ltd
3 Queen Square, London WC1N 3AU
Music drawn by Sambo Music Engraving
Cover design and typography by John Bury
Printed in England

Song of the Volga Boatmen

Melody in F

ANTON RUBINSTEIN

Nocturne from String Quartet No. 2

ALEXANDER BORODIN

Polovtsian Dance (*Prince* I*gor*)

ALEXANDER BORODIN

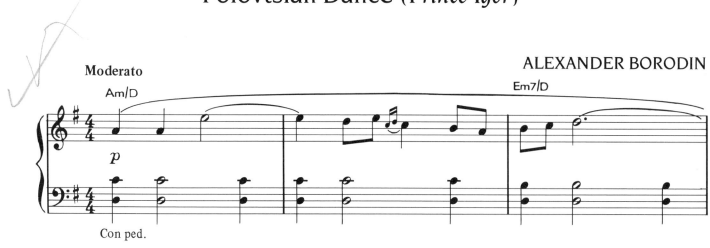

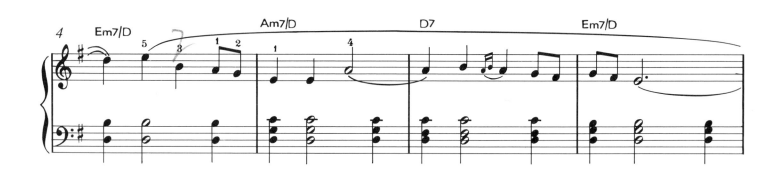

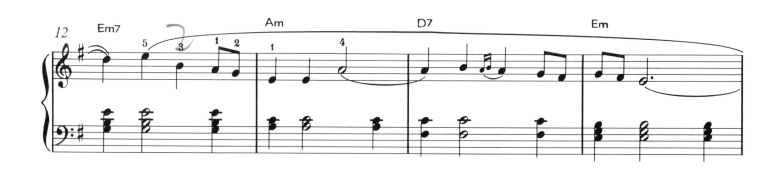

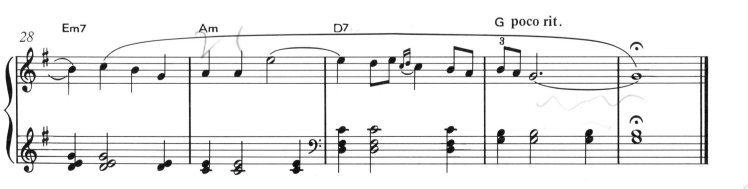

Overture (*Ruslan and Lyudmila*)

MIKHAIL GLINKA

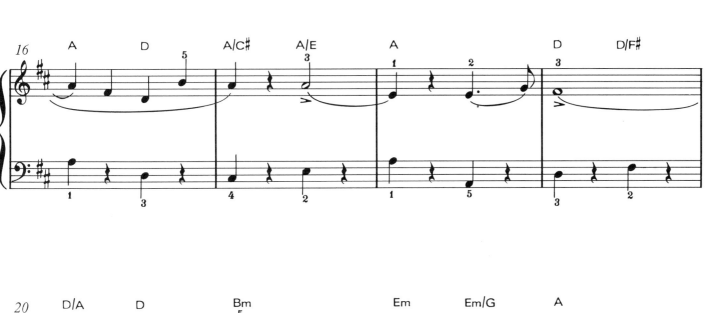

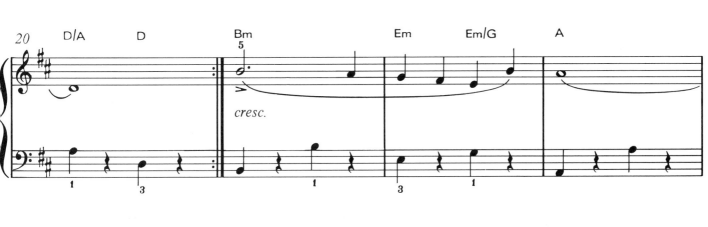

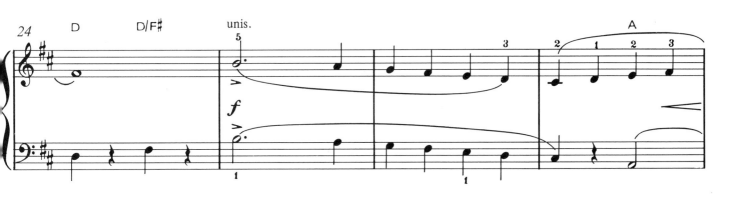

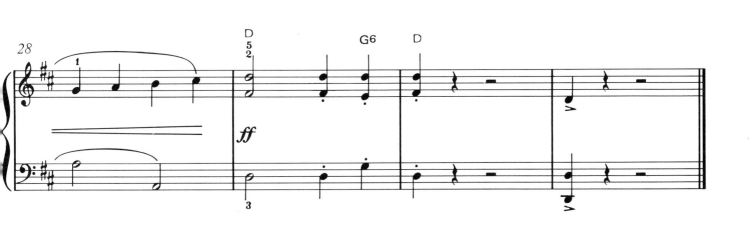

Pictures at an Exhibition

MODEST MUSSORGSKY

PROMENADE

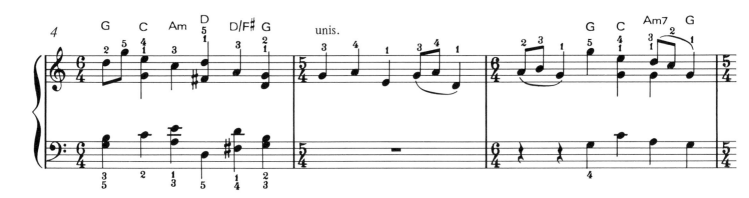

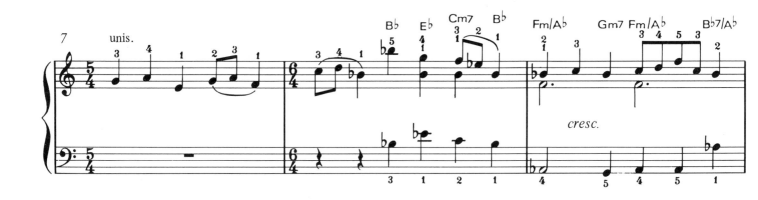

GREAT GATE OF KIEV

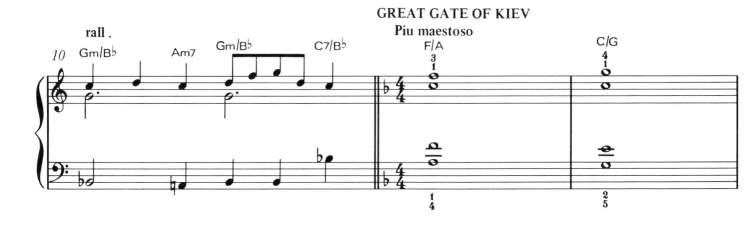

Waltz (*The Sleeping Beauty*)

PYOTR ILYICH TCHAIKOVSKY

Waltz of the Flowers (*The Nutcracker*)

PYOTR ILYICH TCHAIKOVSKY

Dance of the Reed Pipes (*The Nutcracker*)

PYOTR ILYICH TCHAIKOVSKY

Dance of the Sugar Plum Fairy (*The Nutcracker*)

Andante ma non troppo

PYOTR ILYICH TCHAIKOVSKY

Dance of the Little Swans (*Swan Lake*)

PYOTR ILYICH TCHAIKOVSKY

Theme from *Swan Lake*

PYOTR ILYICH TCHAIKOVSKY

Theme from Piano Concerto No. 1

PYOTR ILYICH TCHAIKOVSKY

Slow Movement from Piano Concerto No. 1

PYOTR ILYICH TCHAIKOVSKY

Slow Movement from Symphony No. 4

PYOTR ILYICH TCHAIKOVSKY

Theme from Symphony No. 5

PYOTR ILYICH TCHAIKOVSKY

Theme from Symphony No. 6 (Pathétique)

PYOTR ILYICH TCHAIKOVSKY

Waltz from Serenade for Strings

PYOTR ILYICH TCHAIKOVSKY

Theme from *Romeo and Juliet*

PYOTR ILYICH TCHAIKOVSKY

Canzonetta from Violin Concerto

PYOTR ILYICH TCHAIKOVSKY

A l'église

PYOTR ILYICH TCHAIKOVSKY

2 themes from 1812 Overture

PYOTR ILYICH TCHAIKOVSKY

Theme from *Sheherazade*

NIKOLAY RIMSKY-KORSAKOV

Theme from *Spanish Caprice*

NIKOLAY RIMSKY-KORSAKOV

Theme from Symphony No. 1

VASILY KALINNIKOV

Slow movement from Piano Concerto No. 2

SERGE RAKHMANINOV

Theme from *Spartacus*

ARAM KHACHATURIAN

Theme from *Peter and the Wolf*